THEODATE POPE RIDDLE

MY GODMOTHER

THEODATE POPE RIDDLE

A REMINISCENCE OF CREATIVITY

by
Phyllis Fenn Cunningham
with photographs by
John K. Atticks, III

PHOENIX PUBLISHING
Canaan, New Hampshire

Cunningham, Phyllis Fenn.
  My godmother, Theodate Pope Riddle.

  Includes index.
1. Riddle, Theodate Pope, 1868-1946. 2. Architects—
United States—Biography. I. Title.
NA737.R53C86 1983   720'.92'4 [B]   83-12202
ISBN 0-914016-97-0

Printed in the United States of America

CONTENTS

PREFACE

S INCE PUBLISHING *Hill-Stead Yesterdays* I have discovered that so many fallacies have been circulated about my godmother, Theodate Pope Riddle, that I felt it necessary to write a longer and definitive account about her and her life at Hill-Stead. Widespread misunderstanding about her life, ideals, and creative work, as well as her planning for Hill-Stead, Westover School, Avon Old Farms School, and other buildings, made it seem right to set down the truth, "not for once, but for all time," as Shakespeare said.

The information in this text is accurate to the best of my knowledge and should set the record straight. This has been a labor of love; the only reward I seek is the belief that it may be worthy of her.

Phyllis Fenn Cunningham

Hartford, Connecticut
March 15, 1983

THE MEANING OF JIL

No one knows the meaning of these initials. They appeared on the stationery, cars, and long golden earrings of my godmother, Theodate Pope. They, like her, were mysterious, but in reality they stood for a beautiful and unusual friendship between three persons, my godmother, Theodate Pope; my other godmother and real aunt, Mary Robbins Hillard; and her younger brother, John Hillard.

These cryptic letters were enscribed on the granite tombstone of the young law student, John Hillard, who died at the age of twenty-six of typhoid fever while studying at Yale. He was Theodate's first devoted male friend and to me these initials signify a secret linkage of those three persons whose thoughts were closely interwoven, whose friendship was profound if not mysterious.

P.F.C.

MY GODMOTHER
THEODATE POPE RIDDLE

CHRONOLOGY

1868   *Born February 2, 1868, in Salem, Ohio, to Alfred Atmore and Ada (Brooks) Pope.*

1880   *Changed name from Effie to Theodate.*

1882-88   *Attended Miss Porter's School for Girls in Farmington, Connecticut.*

1884   *Drew up first plans for Hill-Stead.*

1888-89   *Took European trip with parents.*

1901   *Constructed Hill-Stead.*

1903   *Death of John Hillard.*

1908   *Fire destroyed stables at Hill-Stead; one building reconstructed to be used later as the Makeshift Theater.*

1912   *Designed Westover School in Middlebury, Connecticut.*

1913   *Opened architectural office in New York City; discovery of Hill-Stead mastodon; Alfred Atmore Pope died.*

1914   *Started purchasing land for Avon Old Farms School.*

1915   *Escaped from sinking SS Lusitania, spent five and a half hours in water before being rescued.*

1916   *Married John Wallace Riddle on May 6; certified as a registered architect by New York State; designed various homes in Connecticut and New York.*

1918   *Founded Alfred Atmore Pope Foundation.*

1

1920 *Commissioned to design restoration of Roosevelt House in New York City.*

1921 *Ada Brooks Pope died.*

1922 *Commenced construction of Avon Old Farms School; awarded Leoni W. Robinson memorial medal by Architectural Club of New Haven, Connecticut; accompanied husband to Argentina when he was appointed ambassador to that country; experienced second shipwreck en route back from Argentina.*

1925 *Changed name of foundation to Pope-Brooks Foundation, Inc. in memory of both parents.*

1927 *Opened Avon Old Farms School.*

1933 *Certified as registered architect by State of Connecticut.*

1940 *Received diploma and silver medal from Fifth Pan American Congress of Architects held in Montevideo, Uruguay; only woman so honored.*

1941 *John Riddle died December 8.*

1942 *Changed name of Avon Old Farms School to Avon School.*

1945 *Became ill with cancer.*

1946 *Died on August 30, 1946*

Prologue

A T HILL-STEAD, a gracious
white colonial house on a hill in
the small New England town of Farmington, Connecticut, a sundial stands
at the end of the sunken garden. Around its top in old English letters
are inscribed the words: ARS LONGA, VITA BREVIS.

The artist who placed the sundial with its inscription there, the architect who designed the plan of the great house, the lonely young rich
girl who was thwarted in love and motherhood, were all the same person, Theodate Pope. Later she was known as Theodate Pope Riddle, for
she was then the wife of Ambassador John Wallace Riddle. She had many
loves in her life and out of each came a significant contribution to youth
and those who appreciated the arts.

At Hill-Stead which Theodate built at the turn of the twentieth century there was always a sense of tranquility and timelessness. Someone
has said: "Perfect art is effortless," at least to the beholder, and life at
Hill-Stead in those days was an art. One entered from the angry, rushing
world outside to find a kind of blissful unawareness of "the inhumanity
of man towards man," the pettiness, and the futility of constant, unremitting effort. One experienced a sense of having come home, home to a
warm hearth fire, inspiring thoughts, beauty in paintings and music, and
a conviction that someone was near who loved you.

3

"An institution is but the shadow of a single man," and it was the imagination and love Theodate Pope provided which guaranteed the happiness one always experienced at Hill-Stead. One felt it on entering. One forced oneself to leave. It was a veritable Shangri-la and, as in the tale of *Lost Horizon,* those who lived at Hill-Stead never appeared to age. Theodate Pope Riddle always looked the same, regardless of the stretching out of years. This was perhaps because she renewed her youth constantly by her association with young persons. She used her thoughts and imagination with and for them, almost to the exclusion of friends her age.

At times it seemed as though my godmother and Hill-Stead were one, for she brought it into existence, used it as an extension of her outgoing personality. As its mistress, she was unstinting in giving of herself and her hospitality. It was another world, an experience not to be duplicated elsewhere. Indeed, being at Hill-Stead in those days was, as expressed in the Zen philosophy, "a liberation from time."

My Godmother's Ancestry and Youth

MY GODMOTHER's ANCESTOR, on her father's side, was Joseph Pope of Yorkshire, England, who sailed from London in 1634 and settled in Salem, Massachusetts. Her grandparents, Alton and Theodate Morrell (Stackpole) Pope, were Quakers living in Vassalboro, Maine. Her grandfather was a woolen manufacturer there before going to Cleveland, Ohio, where he founded Alton Pope & Sons. His son, Alfred Atmore Pope, my godmother's father, lived in Salem, Ohio, a suburb of Cleveland, next door to Ada Brooks, my godmother's mother. The parents of Ada Brooks were wealthy and did not wish their daughter to associate with a wellborn youth of Quaker ancestry who had little money and no social standing. However, the children paid no heed, they became engaged over the fence, with horsehair rings, at the age of twelve. To earn money and make himself acceptable to the parents of Ada Brooks, young Pope went to work in the Cleveland Malleable Iron Company. Seeing his ability to work hard and earn a living, the parents gave their consent to the marriage. Later, he became president of this firm as well as of the National Malleable Castings Company and other companies. He became richer than the Brookses!

Theodate's Unhappy Childhood

Theodate Pope, my godmother, was born on February 2, 1868, in Salem, Ohio. She endured a desperately unhappy childhood, due to her parents' consuming love for each other. They had no time for their only child, and constantly neglected her, leaving her to the care of indifferent nursemaids and governesses. Having no companions her own age, she read many books and developed a great imagination. Her parents taught her nothing — not even about God. Later, as a teenager at Miss Porter's School, she asked another student: "How do you pray? What do you say to God?"

Her parents, caring nothing for her, gave her the insignificant name of Effie. Later, at age twelve, she rebelled, and insisted that it be changed to 'Theodate' after her grandmother, Theodate Morrell, from Maine. This name in Greek means "Gift of the Gods."

Their shameful neglect was repaid by her—not in kind—but in giving them Hill-Stead, the beautiful home she built in Farmington, Connecticut. She had no bitterness in her heart for them. In spite of their cruelty to her she had love in such abundance that all who knew her or stayed at Hill-Stead benefited by it.

Stockily built, with light brown wavy hair and unusually penetrating deep blue eyes, she had a smile that was full of love for all young persons, and a laugh like the chime of silver bells. She used her incredible imagination to create Hill-Stead, Westover School for girls, and Avon Old Farms School for boys, devoting much of her life to the task.

Portraits of Alfred Atmore Pope and Ada Brooks Pope painted by Arthur Pope, a cousin of Theodate, now hang at Hill-Stead.

Theodate Pope Riddle / 6

2

Building Hill-Stead

Teenage Years at Farmington

MY GODMOTHER's whole life changed when she was sent to Miss Porter's School for Girls in Farmington, Connecticut. It was here that she decided to become an architect, and it was here that she made the enduring friendship with Mary Robbins Hillard, a very young teacher at this school, who was my real aunt as well as my other godmother. My aunt, observing the young girl's loneliness, made an effort to befriend her. Together they took long walks, discussing life, death, art, and ideals. Their favorite road led up the hill from Miss Porter's School to the site on which Hill-Stead now stands. It was during these times that Aunt Theo poured out her ambition to be an architect. She also confided that this was the spot where she would like to build her home. New England freed her, she felt, and she loved the friendly town of Farmington. My Aunt Mary encouraged her and she was soon drawing plans — a giant project for a sixteen-year-old, but she persisted.

Aunt Theo enjoyed the view from the top of her hill where she hoped to build. The house, she decided, should stand facing the west, with a wide front porch from which to see the sunset and distant mountains. In the northwest corner were "The Barn-Door Hills," her favorites.

Back of this site was a high hill. While exploring this, she and my Aunt Mary soon discovered crude stone steps created by the Indians and leading to the top where there was a deep spring. Here would be her water supply! It has never failed, in spite of many guests at Hill-Stead and serious droughts.

She envisioned a New England farm, complete with cows, sheep, pigs, chickens, and an ample vegetable garden. It would be completely self-sufficient, and for the first time in her sixteen years, she felt she had found her home!

Theodate while a student at Miss Porter's School.

Romance entered her life in the 1890s after her graduation from Miss Porter's School. John Hillard, Aunt Mary's younger brother and a Yale law student, was her great love. After he died from typhoid fever, at the age of twenty-six, she postponed marriage until she was forty-nine, and then married a much older man.

Because of John's early death, my two godmothers were stricken with grief and journeyed to Boston for seances with the famous spiritualist, Mrs. Piper, hoping to contact John in the next world. Apparently they had some success, but would never tell about it. Yet because of this Hill-Stead's library has the largest collection of books on spiritualism in the United States.

After her graduation from Miss Porter's School in 1888, her parents gave her a grand tour of Europe, where she was impressed with the "beauty that had been developed through the centuries of culture and tradition." On her return she was not satisfied with the thought of merely being a part of the social life of Cleveland; she wished to live in Farmington and to do something worthwhile with her life. When she obtained her parents' consent, she rented the property of James O'Rourke at Thirteen High

John Hillard's tombstone at Plymouth, Connecticut.

John Hillard at the age of 26.

Street, with the option to buy the house and forty-two acres of land. She later exercised the option and this real estate became the nucleus around which the extensive Hill-Stead estate grew. At first she called this house the O'Rourkerey. In 1896 she was able to purchase the smaller house which stood next to it to the north from Frank and Anna McCahill. She then moved it to join the larger house.

The Gundy and The O'Rourkerey

When she moved into the O'Rourkerey she renamed it the Cottage. The later section which she had joined to it, she called the Gundy, where the girls of Miss Porter's School were welcome to meet, since they had no other place for recreation except their dormitories. The Gundy became popular with the girls who were served tea or chocolate and cookies, and they came in such numbers that many had to sit on the floor. It was here that my godmother opened her "Odds and Ends Shop."

The Cottage was my godmother's home for several years, furnished simply and severely as a farmhouse of the early 1800s would have been, and the girls were encouraged to roam through it so that they could see

Bedroom at Hill-Stead frequently used by John Hillard before his death.

how their ancestors had lived. Aunt Theo loved the old house and even after Hill-Stead had been built she sometimes returned to live in it when she wished to escape pressures and needed to pause and reflect. Friends or relatives were often housed there, and the last to live in the Cottage was her husband's half sister, Grace Flandreau, who died there in January 1972 after a long illness.

Aunt Theo was interested in young persons and their education. She remodeled rooms in the old Farmington Academy and organized classes in sewing and domestic science for local girls, paying the teachers for several years herself. She sponsored the first visiting nurse in Farmington, paying her out of the profits from her "Odds and Ends Shop," proceeds being donated to the Visiting Nurses of Farmington. If there were an insufficient surplus she absorbed the difference personally.

At this time she took an apartment in New York City and worked in Lillian Wald's Henry Street Settlement House, and also in a New York psychiatric clinic. Then, returning to Farmington, she purchased a house called Underledge, which she used as an office. Here she later housed the draftsmen from Stanford White's architectural firm when they came

Theodate and Mary Hillard on the porch of the Gundy during the building of Hill-Stead.

11 / *Building Hill-Stead*

Theodate at the rail of the sunken garden shortly after its completion.

Theodate Pope Riddle / 12

to work on her plans for Hill-Stead.

While my godmother was dreaming about Hill-Stead and drawing preliminary plans, she often wrote to her parents in Ohio, describing the beauties of New England and her special spot. Her father, having made a fortune in malleable steel, felt that Farmington sounded like the place he would like to live when he retired. After visiting his daughter, he decided to finance the Hill-Stead project. With her father's backing assured, Aunt Theo contacted the nation's best known architect, Stanford White, and after explaining how she visualized her future home, he agreed to follow her ideas and plans.

Stanford White's Legacy

The birth and death (1853-1906) of this great man are ephemeral compared with the legacy of beautiful buildings he created. He was also a builder of friendships, and the art of friendship is one often neglected now, in this rushing age of Aquarius, the end of the twentieth century. Stanford White was a giver, and so complete was his enthusiasm and absorption in his work, that it was customary for him to be immersed in

The front facade of Hill-Stead.

some creative project at his office from 7:00 A.M. to 10:00 P.M. Always, he gave his best efforts to whatever he loved: his wife and son, his friends, his work. His genius enabled him to conceive glorious buildings, homes, clubs, churches, railway stations, and even the great East Wing of the White House.

Stanford, like his father, did not follow a chosen career because of finances. His father wanted him to become a musician, and Stanford longed to be an artist, but because artists in those days made little money, Stanford decided on an architectural career. There were no schools for architecture, and he was accepted as a beginning draftsman by Henry Hobson Richardson, the most famous architect of that time.

From this humble beginning White's career climaxed with the formation of the prestigious firm of Mead, McKim & White, whose name was associated with the design and construction of numerous landmark buildings. Thus it was at the peak of White's career that Aunt Theo approached and subsequently engaged him to help her design and build Hill-Stead. From Theodate Pope's own designs and plans, this hill-home evolved, aided by the warmth and genius of Stanford White. He liked

Photograph of Hill-Stead taken by Theodate.

Theodate's bedroom at Hill-Stead.

15 / *Building Hill-Stead*

her ideas well enough to use them, often to the exclusion of his own.

In creating plans for her home, Aunt Theo evolved the innovative idea of insulating the walls with seaweed as did her Quaker ancestors in Maine. This she learned from her Quaker grandmother, Theodate Morrell. Aunt Theo designed walls three feet thick for this purpose and the insulation worked *extremely* well. Hill-Stead is warm in winter, cool in summer, and also quiet; voices in one room cannot be heard in another. Thus Theodate Pope incorporated into Hill-Stead the coziness, the warmth, and the livability of a New England farmhouse, but for the outside, she bowed to White's design, with formal white pillars on the front porch, not unlike Mount Vernon.

The Role of Richard F. Jones

Once the plans were completed, Aunt Theo knew she must find a competent carpenter. When she sent for the three men who had applied for the job, she found that one was drunk and that the second had gone fishing. In desperation, she hired the third, a very young man, Richard F. Jones of Unionville, Connecticut, age twenty. The first buildings he

The Ell-room, where Theodate received her visitors.

constructed at Hill-Stead were the big cattle barns. He did so well with them that he was hired to build what the neighbors called "The Great House" (Hill-Stead).

Russell Jones later wrote about his grandfather as follows:

In later years he would tell of the "eight coats of paint on the inside trim" and how they were applied. He knew where he had put every stud, joist, and header. But his best story concerned a company inevitably referred to as "the big New York plumbing firm." It seems that these worthies protested to Theodate Pope when they learned she had hired some country bumpkin to build the "big house" as everyone called Hill-Stead. They feared delays, lack of skilled cooperation, mistakes, and all kinds of added costs. In some manner Miss Pope calmed their fears and the work proceeded and how! To Miss Pope's great joy this same "big New York plumbing firm" had to ask her to slow down that great young builder because he was going too fast for them!

The success of his work with Miss Pope led to many other contracts: Miss Porter's School, under its able Mistress, Mrs. Keep, "The Elder," was

The "Westover Triumvirate": Mary Hillard, Principal; Helen Dean LaMonte, Assistant Headmistress; and Lucy Baily Pratt, Treasurer.

embarking on an expansive program that provided for Jones the Builder, for fifty years. Many residences in Farmington and later in Hartford were built for clients influenced by the splendor of the work of this master builder. Bushnell Memorial in Hartford is an example.

My godmother also hired him to help her build Westover School in Middlebury, Connecticut, of which my Aunt Mary became headmistress. As a result of that job he was asked to build the Congregational Church on the Green, also in Middlebury. Later he aided my godmother in constructing Avon Old Farms School for boys and then built the Gothic Chapel at Trinity College in nearby Hartford, considered one of the finest examples of Gothic architecture in New England and perhaps the United States.

Hill-Stead Today

Hill-Stead has twenty-eight rooms with fireplaces in many of them, and eleven bathrooms. There are those who say that its proportions are reminiscent of Mount Vernon, others that it is a little like Hyde Park, while some think the setting reminds them of Jefferson's Monticello. It

Robert Brandegee of Farmington painted Theodate in the early 1900s.

has been open as a museum since my godmother's death in 1946. It still has all the original furnishings and paintings, and except for the addition of air conditioning in 1969 it has changed very little. President Theodore Roosevelt, in a letter to his sister, Mrs. Cowles, wife of Admiral William Sheffield Cowles, of Farmington, said: "I shall always be glad you took me to Hill-Stead. It seems to me the ideal of what an American country home should be."

Aunt Theo's will established Hill-Stead as a museum to be kept exactly as she had left it: beds made up; Chippendales and Sheratons dusted; Ming bowls and Barye bronzes polished; Manets, Monets, Degases, Cassatts, and early Whistlers glowing, not on gallery walls, but over fireplaces, rosewood desks, and along staircase walls. These art treasures had been bought by Aunt Theo's father, Alfred Atmore Pope, often before the artist had achieved recognition.

Every bedroom has its bath. All the clocks work—the Louis Quinze with its winking circle of rhinestones, the mahogany grandfather clock in the hall, the Elizabethan water clock made in "Ye olde Towne Yorke"—

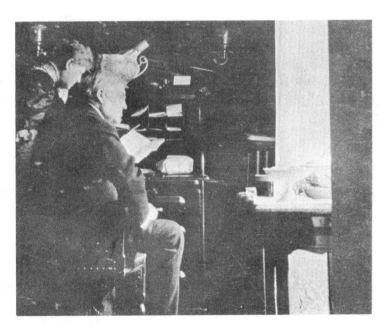

Theodate and her father at Hill-Stead.

are all ticking on time. (The maker of the water clock engraved on it: "Tyme Passeth Swift Away.")

Mr. Pope enjoyed playing on his nine hole golf course which he had laid out on the grounds of Hill-Stead that slope to the pond. Each year he opened it for a little tournament, donating a set of golf clubs as a prize.

Some of the stables were destroyed by fire in 1908, but one building was reconstructed and used as "The Makeshift Theater," a place to be enjoyed by the boys of Avon School for lectures or films. Mr. Riddle's Russian sleigh is here.

Aunt Theo also built some small duplex homes on Garden Street for the Hill-Stead employees and designed the Swedish Gift Shop on Farmington's Main Street.

The Hill-Stead Grounds

While Hill-Stead was being constructed my godmother created a sundial to stand in the Sunken Garden, just south of the house. Made of red sandstone from Talcott Mountain (once a volcano), it is inscribed on the four sides with her cryptic initials: JIL. Around the top in Latin, are the words: ARS LONGA, VITA BREVIS (Art is long; Life is short). At the bottom, often hidden by thick grass, are Old English rhymes: on the north side, facing the house: AMID YE FLOWERS, I TELL YE HOURS; on the east side facing the open side-porch: SO MAN SHALL RISE ABOVE YE SKIES; on the south side, facing the pastures where Aunt Theo had her small studio: BEYOND YE TOMB, FRESH FLOWERS BLOOM; and on the west side, facing Mrs. Pope's wildflower garden: TIME WINGS AWAY, AS FLOWERS DECAY.

The gardenhouse, or gazebo (as it was called in the Sunken Garden), was a meeting place for many guests, and it seemed to augment good conversation. Aunt Theo often loved to sit there alone, on a May morning listening to the birds sing and admiring her specially grafted purple magnolia in bloom. She thought a great deal. Once, she remarked to me: "When I seem laziest then I am the most creative!"

Over the fence from the Sunken Garden, stands the white wooden house where the caretaker and his family live. His daughter's horse enjoyed galloping about the pasture which is next to the house.

In front of the caretaker's house parallel with the Sunken Garden, is the sheep barn, built of fieldstones from Hill-Stead's acres. My godmother believed in using stones and earth from her own land, and her stone fences surrounding her estate are remarkable in their careful construction and strength. The sheep run, which opens from the sheep barn, is built of her own boulders. Across from this stood her garage, housing her Stutz roadster and yellow Packard known as "the Yellow Peril." Opposite the sheep barn was a six stall horse stable. Now converted into the Makeshift Theater, it is used for lectures and films, has pews from an old New England church, and can seat about one hundred persons.

On the west side of the Sunken Garden is the road, lined with stone walls as a protection for the horse pasture. Beyond the horse pasture on the north side is the grass tennis court. Grass courts are rare in this country and the idea originated in England. Grass in this court had to be cut very short, but it was always well cared for by my godmother's devoted helpers.

To the north of this tennis court, standing in front of Hill-Stead's front porch, were many wine glass elm trees. All are dead now except for two that still stand on either side of the house. Below them, on the north, is the animal graveyard where Aunt Theo buried her beloved pets (recounted in a later chapter).

My godmother created a pond at the bottom of her sheep pasture. She called water "the Eye of the Landscape," and one can see this lovely

Art students painting from the front lawn in the early 1960s.

spot from most of the bedrooms. She also needed this pond for ice as there were no refrigerators in those days. The red sandstone icehouse stands across a tiny bridge covering the brook that supplies the pond's water. Beside this icehouse is a tall willow tree, giving the landscape a golden color with its yellow leaves. Back of this is the swamp, with its black bog, in which were found the only known remains of a prehistoric mastodon ever discovered on the East Coast.

At the entrance of Hill-Stead on Farmington Avenue and beyond the pond and big red barns, stands the old farmhouse built in the 1700s by a man named North. Aunt Theo's farmer lived here across from the barns that housed the Jersey cows, pigs, and chickens.

All this was the culmination of a young girl's dream, a beautiful home in a lovely rural setting with a serene view of the distant hills to the west. Once Hill-Stead was completed, Aunt Theo opened her home to a continuous visitation of friends. I was among them and it was here that I was privileged to spend my first night away from home.

Hill-Stead today.

3

My First Visit to Hill-Stead

WHEN I was only a few days old, both my godmothers arrived to visit the infant. Still stunned by the early death of young John Hillard, they looked down at me. Aunt Theo said: "She has the same look in her eyes that John had when he died!" From that moment, they took me into their hearts.

Aunt Theo gave me my name. "Phyllis goes well with Fenn," she told my mother. She also advised my parents not to give me a middle name. "She will doubtless marry," said my godmother, "and a middle name would not be practical. Just name her 'Phyllis Fenn.' Do you know what Phyllis means in Greek? 'A green bough.' This signifies that she will never grow old."

My First Night Away From Home

When I was eight years old, I spent my first night away from home at Hill-Stead. It was June and Aunt Theo thought I would enjoy my first ride in an open trolley that ran between Hartford and Farmington. At the road that led to Hill-Stead, my godmother's faithful chauffeur met us and drove us to the house, after which he took my mother home to Hartford.

For sleeping accommodation my godmother gave me a small room at the top of the second floor stairs, and she moved into the little bedroom next to mine in case I might be homesick. I was— *Terribly*! I can remember that first night when sleep would not come for thinking of my home and what my mother and father were doing. I pictured them sitting, as they always did, by the brass lamp in our living room in Hartford, reading aloud, and I wept, remembering.

When at last I had cried out my grief and was ready for sleep, I

Snapshot of the author at her home in Hartford
taken by Aunt Theo in 1913.

Theodate Pope Riddle / 24

saw the door to my bedroom open quietly, and in came Aunt Theo. After looking at me lovingly (I pretended to be asleep), she shut my door very softly and then went into her room next door.

Turning over my wet pillow I tried to sleep for it was very late, one o'clock, so the diamond studdied clock read on the mantelpiece in my room. It ticked and ticked, and I found that the ticks kept waking me, so, crawling out of my bed, I carefully lifted this priceless clock and laid it face down on the hearth. It stopped ticking. Getting back into my bed, I slept till five or until the rooster began to crow and the sun to rise. Then, thinking of my home again, I began to weep.

Suddenly, the door between our rooms opened, and Aunt Theo called, "Come into my room and I'll read to you!" I did. She read a poem called "The Jolly Goshawk" from *The Book of English Ballads.* I shall never forget it, and that book is still there at Hill-Stead in that same bedroom!

Soon, I was happy and ready to go down to an early breakfast in the dining room. We had Scotch oatmeal covered with brown sugar, and cream so thick that we had to spoon it from the pitcher! This was from

The dining room.

The bed in which the author spent her first night in Hill-Stead.

Aunt Theo's famous Jersey cow named Anesthasia, Pride of Hill-Stead. Then there were eggs and bacon from her own farm, muffins or toast with marmalade, and rich milk for me.

After breakfast it was time for me to go into the butler's pantry, where the devoted butler, Ernest, was feeding Silas, the white, shorthaired dog that became my constant companion. He followed me everywhere.

I loved to take Silas for a walk after breakfast down the grassy hill to the little pond (where later I caught my first fish) and to see the sheep pastured near it in a lovely peaceful meadow filled with June grass, daisies, and buttercups. Silas liked to bark at the sheep and I delighted in chasing them. They were so brainless, I thought, always following their leader and never thinking for themselves. It was then that I decided to be an individual, *not* a sheep, and I've been one ever since.

At lunchtime we sat on the side porch to eat a sumptuous meal, after which, in the long, unhurried, summer afternoons, I would play in the sunken garden or ride the fat brown pony named Brandy.

I always enjoyed teatime because of the rock sugar Aunt Theo used instead of the conventional lump of sugar. Tea tasted enchanting, even

The small guest bedroom was usually reserved for young, overnight visitors.

The author in her late teens during the period of Westover houseparties at Hill-Stead.

my "cambric tea" with a large crystallized piece of sugar at the bottom of my cup. In the sugar bowl it resembled a large uncut diamond.

We always wore evening dress for dinner which was a formal meal. Candles, tall and graceful, lit the table; a hearth fire crackled in the fireplace; and gourmet food was served by the two butlers. After we were all seated (Aunt Theo often invited adult guests for dinner), Ernest, the first butler, would enter bearing a huge silver platter of fish or meat. Bowing, he held it for a moment before Aunt Theo, and after she had nodded her head in approval, he would begin to pass it to the guests. I often wondered what would happen if she shook her head, but she never did. Wine was served to the adults with each course, in tiny wineglasses, usually three or four lined up beside the water goblets.

When I reached the age of twelve and visited Hill-Stead, my bedroom was changed from the small one upstairs to the large bedroom on the first floor called by New Englanders "the Parlor Bedroom."

It had a huge four-poster bed hung with drapes and an elegant bathroom with a marble sink and a deep tub. This room also had an antique bureau with cut glass jars, tortoiseshell-backed combs and brushes, a buttonhook, and an ornately framed mirror. In a corner by the door was a large Jacobean desk with secret drawers. Opposite, in the other corner back of the door, was the pastel by Degas entitled *The Tub*. It faced the bed and showed a slim naked girl standing in a small white tub, bending over to wash her feet. Since I have posed for artists, I now know that the model for this pastel was a dancer, as no one but a dancer could hold so difficult a pose for twenty minutes (the normal time for an artist to use a model between rest periods). On the mantel over the fireplace stood a rhinestone decorated clock; to the right of this was an oil portrait of Isadora Duncan by Carrière. Under this, on a small mahogany table, was a pink porcelain vase filled with dried rose petals. Beside the bed stood a small table with a crystal-pendant lamp, back of which another mirror gleamed.

I might add that a few years ago *The Tub* was moved to the living room. Why? Was it because the sight of this charming girl disturbed the sleep of those guests who were privileged to sleep in "the Parlor Bedroom"?

To return to my childhood, after a late dinner, at eight o'clock, which did not end until around nine thirty, I retired while Aunt Theo took the men of the party to the library for brandy, leaving the women to chatter in the Ell Room.

Being always curious, as soon as I was ready for bed I would open my heavy door to the library (just a crack) and, lying on the floor, listened for hours to the male guests' erudite discussions of fascinating subjects. It was right then that I decided *men* were the most interesting persons in the human race, and that *women* were only a necessary evil.

Helpers at Hill-Stead

Ernest, the mulatto butler whom I mentioned previously, purchased the food for the help, who had their own cheerful dining room where they had breakfast at seven, coffee at ten, lunch at twelve, tea at two, and dinner at six. Every Friday, Ernest procured fish and also beer for their dinner. They were well fed, happy, and completely devoted to my godmother.

Ernest was the most faithful of all the help. He refused to leave Hill-Stead to take a vacation, he loved it so much. One day Aunt Theo called for him and said: "Ernest, you haven't had a vacation since you arrived here three years ago! I think you should take one."

"Very well, madame, if you wish it," he replied.

After he was gone three days he returned in tears and reported to my godmother: "I *can't* be away from Hill-Stead! I was unhappy all those three days, and I wish only to stay here—all the time—for the rest of my life!" He did just that and died after sixty-two years of service. He

The staff at Hill-Stead in 1900.

Theodate Pope Riddle / 30

is buried beside Aunt Theo in the cemetery by the Farmington River.

Her personal maid, Annie Jacobs, stood by her also, but her secretary, Miss Elizabeth McCarthy, was with her from the first to the last, and then lived in her own house in Farmington until her death in 1981. When introducing Miss McCarthy to a famous person Aunt Theo said: "She is the *sweetest* little secretary! I couldn't do without her! She's always there when I need her. She never complains. She is very competent!"

A number of other helpers were neeeded to run the large estate: a gardener, a stableman, a sheep herder, a driver, a houseman, a laundress, and a number of maids. I still remember Patrick Flood, the genial houseman who did errands for Aunt Theo; Harry Loomis, always in his snappy uniform, who drove her Rolls-Royce and Stutz cars; Thompson, the other attentive butler; and Mary Heeny and Maria Quinlan, two of the many maids who came and went over the years.

To a twelve-year-old it seemed as though my godmother had a huge retinue of servants but they were all necessary for such an establishment. Aunt Theo needed all of them, not only to help entertain the continual parade of guests, but also because the household soon grew to include three active foster sons who managed to keep those helpers very busy indeed!

Ernest, Dandy, and the pony cart.

Ernest.

4

Children and Pets at Hill-Stead

HILDREN AND PETS go together,
and this was certainly true at Hill-
Stead where the young people had absolute freedom to wander through
the fields and pastures and they made friends with all the animals. It was
almost as though Aunt Theo had consciously prepared for this special rela-
tionship in anticipation of the time when she would bring children into
her home.

Hurdy-gurdy at Hill-Stead and the monkey fascinates Silas the dog,
Gordon Brockway, the Ambassador, and servants alike.

Children at Hill-Stead

Aunt Theo, destined never to have children of her own, fostered three sons, the first of whom was a year-old baby. Inviting me to accompany her when she went to meet the train which was bringing this child from a Boston orphanage, her eyes filled with tears of joy as the matron put the darling little boy into her arms.

Gordon Brockway was a beautiful child: he had bright golden curls, deep blue eyes, and a loving disposition. He developed a great affection for my godmother, and she loved him as though he were her very own and cared for him in every way. Her secretary, Miss McCarthy, told me: "Gordon could never be spoiled — no matter how much you did for him. He was a *perfect* child!" Too perfect, perhaps, because at age four he contracted polio although there had not been a case in or near Farmington. He died, and Aunt Theo told me she would never get over the pain of losing him. She said: "Now I know how other mothers feel when they lose a son."

Her other two foster sons were Paul Martin (from New Orleans) who had been deserted by his parents and left in an orphanage, desolate and

Gordon Brockway.

Gordon Brockway watches
John Alsop and Brandy.

unhappy, and Donald Carson, whose parents, both missionaries in South Africa, had died. These boys were about twelve years old when Aunt Theo brought them to Hill-Stead, and they became my constant companions as we were the same age. John Alsop, who was from Avon and also our age, visited often. He was a godson of Aunt Theo's and is now past-president of the Board of the Covenant Insurance Company in Hartford.

Aunt Theo never said to me: "You *must* do this—because all the other children are doing it!" At Hill-Stead she let each of us grow up in our own way, and yet she never had any disciplinary problems with the young persons she fostered or sheltered in her unique home.

Aunt Theo also took in André Maximov, a teenager who had escaped from Russia during the Russian Revolution. He stayed at Hill-Stead for several years until he decided to become a lawyer, and Aunt Theo financed his education at law school. He became a successful attorney in New York City and married a beautiful dancer. When he first arrived at Hill-Stead, he gave us great joy and happiness with his piano playing. Each day and often during the evening he would play works of Chopin, Rachmaninoff, and many other composers for Aunt Theo and her guests. Aunt Theo's

Paul Martin tests his bicycle
at Hill-Stead.

Yum-Yum.

Theodate Pope Riddle / 34

favorite piece was the Chopin Étude, opus 10, in E major. Whenever I hear it now, I mentally see Hill-Stead in the evening, with soft lights, and Aunt Theo sitting in the Ell Room, gazing out the window, her long golden earrings, with the initials, JIL, swinging as she moved. This composition seemed to express the tranquility and beauty of Hill-Stead in those halcyon days.

Her foster sons, Paul and Donald, married and left for distant places. One wrote to her during his honeymoon. After reading his letter, she had tears in her eyes and said to me: "There is *nothing* like young love!"

When I married and moved to another state with my doctor husband, Aunt Theo found Dolly Rutledge from the South to take my place in helping entertain the Avon School masters and boys, but Dolly soon married and left.

How *lucky* we were! Those of us who, as children or teenagers, enjoyed the experience of living or visiting at Hill-Stead!

Pets at Hill-Stead

Pets at Hill-Stead were treated as though they were human beings. Such love and care were showered upon them! Because of this they responded to my godmother with love and we at Hill-Stead, in those happy days, had many animals surrounding us. There was the Shetland pony, Brandy, that drew us in his cart along the wooded roads near Hill-Stead. Then there were the sheep which grazed in the pasture and which we liked to chase, until Aunt Theo forbade it, saying that the lamb chops were made tough because of this custom. Thereafter we merely petted the sheep. A special pet was the fierce parrot that perched on Aunt Theo's shoulder, warning difficult guests to keep at a distance. More than once I saw this parrot nip a belligerent houseguest. Two Persian cats roamed the rooms, loyal only to Aunt Theo, allowing no one else to caress them. The two chow dogs sat adoringly at her feet and would pay no heed to anyone else. And there was my favorite, Silas, the white-and-black terrier that adopted me and followed me everywhere.

Silas was so devoted to me that one time he tried to accompany me to Hartford when my mother came to take me back on the open trolley that ran between Hartford and Farmington. The chauffeur drove us to the trolley station where we sat and waited until the trolley came rushing around the curve. Then my mother pushed me on and climbed in beside me, while the chauffeur handed us my bags and helped pile them near us.

Just before the conductor clanged the bell to start, I felt something

The Hill-Stead parrot, friend of some, fierce foe of many.

nudging my legs. Looking down, I saw Silas snuggled close under my seat.

"Mother! Silas wants to go to Hartford with me. *Can* he?"

"Oh, dear, *no!*" exclaimed my mother. "Conductor! Conductor! Will you please wait a moment? We have a *dog* under our seat. We *can't* take him to Hartford!"

Instantly, the good conductor was by our side trying valiantly to dislodge Silas. The poor man hauled and pulled and coaxed and swore and finally said:

"This will delay our trip at least fifteen minutes! I may lose my job! And all because of this *dog!*" At last, he got poor Silas out and into the waiting arms of the faithful chauffeur.

As the trolley rolled away, I looked back and could see my devoted pet scrambling and whining, longing to follow me, the chauffeur having a difficult time holding him back.

Other pets we children had were the Jersey cows: patient, gentle creatures, mooing and chewing their cuds. I enjoyed petting them, and often watched them being milked in the huge red barns. (The color of these barns, a true New England tone, was obtained by mixing red pigment with sour milk.) The bull was a creature to be wary of. Proud and hefty, he stood in the pasture, king of the cows. Once, one of Aunt Theo's foster sons dared me to pet this fierce bull, and since I've always taken a dare, I did so this time. Climbing over the tall stone wall, I petted the nose of this bull as he stood glaring at me with his small, rather red eyes. As I did so, he let out a wild bellow and began to chase me. Luckily, I was near the wall and climbed over it quickly. The foster son patted me on the back, remarking: "You're a good sport, Phyllis, but never tell Aunt Theo I made you do this!"

The sheep were a delight, and we petted them in their sheepfold — a kind of stone walled corral where they spent the night, and we even learned how to bleat as they did. The lambs were so soft and wobbly on their legs and so unafraid of us that we loved to hold them in our arms.

Aunt Theo's concern for her animals at Hill-Stead continued after they had died. She had an animal graveyard at the foot of her hill. One goes down a thicket path to a small plot of land sheltered on one side by a giant pine tree and on the other by a large maple tree. This plot holds small gravestones, carved from the red sandstone of Talcott Mountain. Each stone has the name of the beloved pet carved on its side. "Ali Baba" is there; also "Brandy," the pony; "Chang" and "Ching," the two chow dogs; and "Silas." Finally there is a marker for "Anesthasia, Pride of Hill-Stead," the Jersey cow who gave us such endless rich milk and cream.

Headstones in the animal graveyard at Hill-Stead.

5

Holidays at Hill-Stead

GUESTS who had never met before at Hill-Stead would greet each other with outstretched hands, saying: "I'm Mrs. Jones. Who are you?" My godmother believed that a guest of hers was a friend to all and that no formal introductions were necessary. Most were older than I, but this seemed to make no difference; we were all congenial, all happy to be there together. Often Aunt Theo would ask me to bring a few girls from Hartford who were my age as companions to her foster sons and the Avon School boys. My friends loved to be invited to Hill-Stead during the holidays and would inquire anxiously: "But *what* shall I wear?" To which I'd say, "Evening clothes, of course. The most colorful you have!"

Aunt Theo was accustomed to leaving for a late dinner at a friend's house in Farmington, letting us young people have Hill-Stead to ourselves, and this was delightful! First, she would seat us at the dinner table, then kiss me an affectionate good-bye, and say: "Have a good time, dear, and if you need anything, you know you can call Ernest. I hope you'll like the dinner!" Then she would leave on her husband's arm, looking radiant in one of her evening gowns, made especially for her, after her own design. She always wore white when she was happiest, and that lovely, simple dress is still hanging in her closet at Hill-Stead.

Christmas at Hill-Stead

At Christmastime, Aunt Theo gave parties for the Farmington children, complete with gifts on the Christmas tree and delectable refreshments. At this season she also had her chauffeur deliver food to the needy in Farmington, with instructions that he never divulge the name of the giver. During World War I she gave constantly to the village poor, anonymously.

Meanwhile, at Hill-Stead the Christmas season, as I remember it nostalgically, was full of a warm and genial hospitality seldom experienced today. Red was the dominant color, Aunt Theo's favorite, and it was everywhere: not in the decorations specifically but in the general feeling that " 'Tis the season to be jolly!" as the old English carol says. The tall Christmas tree in the dining room was lavishly covered with dangling, sparkling ornaments brought from many lands. There were Christmas wreathes, mistletoe, and holly over the doors, while poinsettias stood on the tables. Pine branches were woven around the banisters, and fires burned on the generous hearths.

New Year's Festivities

New Year's was a time to be happily remembered at Hill-Stead. At dinner the large dining table was so crowded with adults that Aunt Theo had little tables set in the Ell Room and living room, for all her young relatives and their friends who came from the Middle West for

View through the library centers on James McNeill Whistler's famous painting "The Blue Wave" hanging over the fireplace mantel.

the celebration. Most of them were teenagers like myself, and I remember one boy who kept close to me, even changing places so he could sit beside me, remarking: "I'll see you in four years, and then I'll ask you to marry me!"

When all the guests were seated, in came the two butlers, dressed in medieval costumes, marching to the blare of a trumpet, carrying on their shoulders a mammoth platter on which reposed a roast suckling pig, complete with an apple in his mouth! I have *never* tasted such meat in my life! Tender, juicy, and how we ate!

After a magnificent repast we would roll up the carpets in the dining room and dance the year out. As the clocks in the house struck midnight, Aunt Theo would raise her hand, and we would all form a circle and sing "Auld Lang Syne." Weaving around, grapevine fashion, we shook each other's hands, saying: "Happy New Year!" While we were doing this, Aunt Theo and Uncle John Riddle sat on the red sofa in the dining room, holding hands and looking at each other with great devotion.

The next day there would be skating on the little pond, and then a hasty packing for home and school.

The conversation corner of the library, where Theodate gathered her distinguished guests for after-dinner brandy and conversation.

Interesting Personalities

The persons I met there, old and young, I have seldom seen since, but fragments of their personalities remain with me. There were the two foster sons, so very courteous, such fun to be with, so rather shy, yet always my friends. I still remember the pale Russian boy who bowed over adults' hands, kissing them ceremoniously. I once remarked to Paul, the eldest of Aunt Theo's foster sons, "Oh, I can't *wait* to be old enough to have André kiss my hand!" Paul laughed. "You'll be old, then, too, ninny!" he said.

Then there was the thirty-year-old young man who took life very seriously and thought us all "very young and very foolish!" He used to sit with Aunt Theo for hours telling her what a state this world was in, and of how he dreamed the world should be! I never kept track of him after my Hill-Stead days, but rumor has it that he shot himself.

Aunt Theo was also very fond of a colonel and his wife, a charming, debonair couple with a great zest for life. They had built a most enchanting one-story house on the very top of a nearby mountain, and I went there once to spend the night when there was no room for me at Hill-Stead. Aunt Theo often invited this couple to Hill-Stead. She so loved to talk with them and hear tales the colonel would tell of his army experiences in faraway places.

The only person whom I disliked at Hill-Stead was a proud woman who used to sweep into the living room after having been announced by the meticulous butler, Ernest. She always wore makeup, unusual in those days — at least to *me* — and she always wore gowns with long trains. She enjoyed dominating her poor, meek husband, who ingratiatingly followed her everywhere. She never would let him speak his mind nor give any opinion without pouncing upon him and refuting what he had said. I once asked him what he did in life, and he (with his only smile I had ever seen on his face) remarked: "I go big game hunting in Africa."

One time, before dinner, this woman got her comeuppance. We were all standing together, Aunt Theo and her guests and I, when Ernest announced her arrival and she swept in with her customary royal manner, wearing a gown with a long train. Effusively she greeted Aunt Theo, kissing her on both cheeks, while Aunt Theo remarked, as she always did to this woman: "My! How *well* you are looking!"

Suddenly all of us became aware that the long train was hitched up in the back — caught by her belt — and showing that she had just been to the bathroom and had forgotten to pull down her skirts.

There was a moment of hushed embarrassment. Then Aunt Theo ran around to the back of this woman and, pulling down her skirts and train, burst out laughing. We all felt we could laugh with impunity, and we did, uproariously. Quickly dinner was announced. We went into the dining room to the always delicious dinner and no more was said of it. As I sipped the consommé, garnished with lemon and parsley, I gloated. Mrs. X, however, never lost her composure. She was made of marble, I am sure.

Mrs. X was as much a part of that now nostalgic era and way of life as Aunt Theo, but fortunately for all of us my godmother did not number many such women among her ever widening and shifting circle of friends.

6

The Hill-Stead Mastodon

ONE SUMMER DAY in 1913 my godmother was eating lunch on the ample side porch with her guests when a workman came rushing to her. Wiping his forehead he said:

"I beg your pardon, Miss Pope, for interrupting your luncheon, but we workmen have discovered something very strange in the earth where we've been digging!"

"Yes? And please won't you tell us what you have found?" asked my godmother.

"Some very big bones! Bigger than I've ever seen, and longer than those of an elephant. I tell you, they give me the creeps!"

"Thank you for coming to tell me," replied my godmother. "We'll all come with you at once to see them!"

Leaving their delicious lunch, they followed the workman in my godmother's old Rolls-Royce. The workman indicated a spot in the swamp where a trough was being dug. My godmother and her guests left the car and managed to walk over rough land and through briers.

The excavated earth was jet black, as the place was part of a peat bog. The long, sharp bones, protruding in the summer light, were mysterious and awesome. My godmother trembled with excitement. Seeing her superintendent among the onlookers, she begged him to call Yale University at once and report this discovery to its Anthropology Department.

Following her orders, Allen Cook was met with disbelief and derision by the Yale anthropologists and scientists.

"*Impossible!*" they said laughing. "You can't be serious! A prehistoric creature buried in Farmington, Connecticut? Ho! Ho! You must be *crazy!* Sorry, but we can't and won't believe you until we see a specimen."

Undaunted, Allen Cook, with Aunt Theo's permission, took a vertebra and drove to Yale's Peabody Museum.

Flabbergasted at the sight of this mammoth ancient bone, Yale sent some specialists to Hill-Stead to treat what they pronounced to be a prehistoric mastodon, the only one ever to be found in New England, or maybe the continent.

In my many years at Hill-Stead after this event no one would ever tell me where these bones were hidden. One man who worked in the fields told me that they had been crated and stored in the garage. My godmother would only smile and shake her head when I inquired of her. She had planned to create a museum for the mastodon at her Avon School but it was never built.

Years later, after my godmother's death, someone said that these bones had been stored at the Avon School. Journeying there, I saw in the headmaster's office a few huge bones sitting on a high bookcase. Asked what they were, he replied: "I really don't know *whose* bones they are! Possibly one of the headmasters who got fired!"

When my son was six years old, I took him to Yale's Peabody

The swampy area on the Hill-Stead grounds where the bones of the mastodon were found.

Museum. There we viewed a mastodon and other primitive fossils. As I was telling him about the Hill-Stead mastodon and its mysterious disappearance, an old guard hobbled over to us.

"Excuse me," he said, "but I heard you mention the Hill-Stead mastodon. Well, *I* was one of the men from Yale who helped get those bones excavated, and I took the great tusk in a taxicab all the way to New Haven to be treated, with this great bone sticking out of the windows of that cab!" (Was this just a mastodon tale invented to amuse and delight a six-year-old boy? I shall never know!)

Now, after years of mystery as to their whereabouts, these same bones are mounted and safe in The American Indian Archaelogical Museum in Washington, Connecticut. My godmother would be happy to see them there!

Part of the Hill-Stead mastodon bones.

7

Famous Visitors

MY AUNT THEO often asked me to invite a few of my girl friends for dinner or luncheon at Hill-Stead, when I was in my teens, and Avon Old Farms School had opened. Many of the younger masters enjoyed coming to Hill-Stead for meals and visits with Aunt Theo. Therefore, Aunt Theo was "long" on boys and "short" on girls. One reason I was popular in Hartford was because all my friends hoped they would be invited to Hill-Stead, so that they forced themselves to be extra kind and cordial to me. Of course, not all were asked. Aunt Theo relished lively conversation, and in those days most Hartford girls lacked the ability to be spontaneously amusing. Many (I realize now) were just plain *dull!*

Katharine Hepburn

Katharine Hepburn was *never* dull! She was a "must" for Hill-Stead. She and I attended the same dances at The Hartford Golf Club and were equally "cut in" by the boys. She, also like me, wore *no* make up. We both scorned it, but she went further in this. Her face always shone like the sun. When I asked her how she accomplished this, she replied, in the now world-famous Hepburn accent, "Oh — I wash my face with sink-soap and then let it dry."

When I asked her to Hill-Stead for dinner, I forgot to inform her that evening clothes were de rigueur. She appeared wearing a short brown velveteen dress with long sleeves and a high neckline.

As she entered the living room (Ernest the butler announcing her) and walked in wearing low-heeled shoes to greet Aunt Theo, the rest of us watched with some apprehension. Aunt Theo paid no heed to the clothes Katharine was wearing, but shook her hand cordially, and soon we were all ushered into the dining room. Now all of us suddenly felt overdressed beside Katharine, who wore her "wrong costume" so gallantly.

Katherine Hepburn as photographed by Gertrude Kasebier
in the Latin Quarter in Paris, c. 1925.

Théodate Pope Riddle / 48

A few days later I was invited to lunch at Hill-Stead. Aunt Theo took me aside and inquired: "And who was your charming young friend of yesterday? I forget her name, but she surely has a *flare* for clothes!"

The Three American Expatriates

Three world famous American expatriates were connected with Hill-Stead: Mary Cassatt, Henry James, and James McNeil Whistler. Two were of similar ages. Henry James was only one year older than Mary Cassatt; he was born in 1843 and she in 1844. Whistler was the oldest, born in 1834. He was the only one who did not visit Hill-Stead because he never returned to this country after he left in 1855 at the age of twenty-one. Henry James spent three months at Hill-Stead, and Mary Cassatt visited often.

These three met and knew each other in Paris and London. Whistler painted a portrait of Mary Cassatt, and Henry James covered Whistler's trial. Cassatt and Whistler were not truly appreciated in this country nor in Europe during their lifetimes. Two of them received prizes: Mary Cassatt, the French Legion of Honor; Henry James, the Order of Merit from the king of England, after he became a British subject late in life. Whistler received no prizes during his lifetime.

All three were completely devoted to their art and were dedicated workers. Whistler died first at the age of sixty-nine. Henry James lived to be seventy-three and died in London. Mary Cassatt lived the longest, until 1926, attaining the age of eighty-two. She died at her Château de Beaufresne in France.

Mary Cassatt

Mary Cassatt, illustrious American painter of mothers and children, met the Popes through the Harris Whittemores of Naugatuck, Connecticut, who invited her to stay at their home while she painted portraits of their children. The Whittemores were a wealthy family and became collectors of art as did the Popes and the Henry O. Havemeyers, who were from New York City. Mary Cassatt became the Havemeyers' agent, traveling with them through Europe and assisting them in building their collection. She was the only American expatriate who helped the Impressionists in France and elsewhere to sell their work in this country.

Mr. Pope bought several Cassatt paintings, but only two hang at Hill-Stead now: a large, beautiful oil of a mother and two children and an aquatint. Both are in a bedroom at Hill-Stead. Mr. Pope liked to buy his Impressionist paintings in Paris, either directly from the artists or from an agent there, either Vincent Van Gogh's brother, Theodore, or Durand-Ruel. He bought many paintings around 1889: two Monet *Haystacks; The Bay at Antibes* (Monet), and Manet's *Toreadors and Olympia,* plus three Degases—*The Dancers, The Jockeys* (both in oil), and *The Tub* (a pastel). Mr. Pope had just acquired the Monet painting, *Ships Leaving the Harbor,* and was staying at the Windsor Hotel in New York City when the hotel suddenly caught fire. Mr. Pope, quickly arranging with firemen to bring this huge painting down a ladder, stood on the sidewalk and watched the precarious descent of his precious painting.

It was through the Whittemores and the Popes that Mary Cassatt met Mary Robbins Hillard and learned of the joint efforts of Theodate Pope and Mary Hillard to create the Westover School for girls.

In Paris, where Mary Cassatt made her home, she wrote both Mrs. Pope and her daughter, Theodate, whom Mary Cassatt called "My dearest young friend." (Mary Cassatt was twenty years older.)

10 Rue de Marignan, Paris
February 18 (no year)

Dear Mrs. Pope:
I have just had a delightful surprise: a visit from Miss Pope. She wrote me saying that she was in Paris with Miss Hillard and this afternoon they were here, and we had a good talk, but not half long enough. Now that she has gone, I think of a hundred things I should have liked to know, and wish I had spoken of. Still, I did have something. That you are delighted with Farmington and are both well is good to know. Miss Pope looked remarkably well.

Handwritten letters from Mary Cassatt are at Hill-Stead, and I quote from two more of them:

December 23, 1910

Dear Theodate:
I need not ask you if you believe in telepathy, but it seemed to me an added proof when your letter reached me here. My family landed on November 24, and ever since then every day we have talked of you and Mary Hillard and your joint effort for the School. (I could not remember the name, but names always escape me). But my sister mentioned it in connection with the daughter of a friend from Philadelphia. This child is wild about the School. One can see what Miss Hillard can do with girls, from the report. Isn't it splendid to be able to influence whole generations!

After Theodate Pope's miraculous rescue from the *Lusitania,* Miss Cassatt wrote her the following letter, dated July 1915, Paris.

My dear dear Theodate:
What an awful experience you have had. If you were saved it is because you have still something to do in this world.

Your affectionate friend,
Mary Cassatt.

Mary Cassatt was born on May 23, 1844, in Allegheny City, Allegheny County, Pennsylvania. Her family moved from place to place all during her childhood and even went abroad for an extended stay. In one of the places where they lived there were horses and Mary learned to ride. She rode superbly and could also drive tandem with great ability. One of her best paintings is entitled *Woman and Child Driving* (1880) and shows a carriage with a mother driving her child while the groom sits behind. She loved animals and always had a horse and many dogs (the latter, mostly Belgian griffons).

Mary Cassatt at tea in her studio in Paris with Mary Hillard in the early 1900s.

This oil, "Mother and Child," and a single watercolor are
the only Mary Cassatt paintings left at Hill-Stead.

When she was twenty, she told her father, a businessman, that she wished to be an artist. He responded tersely: "I'd rather see you dead!" She persisted and finally went abroad to study and paint, having a studio in Paris and, later, a château in Oise, France.

Studying under Corregio, she was friends with Degas, Manet, Monet, Pissaro, Matisse, Renoir, Berthe Morisot (the only other woman in this Impressionist group), and Sisley. She also had a good friend in the premier of France, Clemenceau, who awarded her, late in her life, the French Legion of Honor.

Always immaculately dressed in the latest fashion, she was tall, slim, erect, and made a striking figure in any gathering with her large feathered or flowered hats set on her light brown wavy hair, her blue-gray eyes sparkling.

She was happiest, it seemed, in her Château de Beaufresne le Mesnil-Theribus, Oise, France. She still had her studio in Paris but spent the best of the year in the country. Here, she not only had her animals but also her devoted servants. Mathilde, her maid, was with her for forty-two years and was there when she died. Her chauffeur, Armand de la Poste, was with her also, and she died resting on his arm.

The end of her life was sad: she went partially blind and could not see to paint. Her old friend, Degas, was slowly dying of old age and going blind. She was much alone, but this did not dishearten her. She kept up to the very end and died at Beaufresne, in June 1926, at the age of eighty-three. She was not truly recognized in either Europe or the United States until after her death, but she lived a very happy life and enjoyed it. Her optimism helped her over the bad parts. Her epitaph should have been: "One Who Greatly Loved."

Henry James

Henry James, the great American expatriate and writer, who spent most of his life in England, wrote of Hill-Stead in his book, *The American Scene,*

A great new house on a hill-top that overlooked the most composed of communities (Farmington, Connecticut), —a house apparently conceived and with the greatest felicity —on the lines of a magnificent Mt. Vernon, and in which an array of modern "Impressionistic" pictures, mainly French, wondrous examples of Manet, Degas, of Claude Monet, of Whistler, of other rare recent hands, treated us of the momentary effect of a large slippery sweet inserted, without a warning, between the compressed lips of half-concious inanition.

One hadn't known one was starved, but the morsel went down by the mere
authority of the consummately prepared!. . .It made everything else fade:
It was like the sudden thrill of a nightingale, lord of the hushed evening.

In the summer of 1911 Henry James spent some time at Hill-Stead.
He was not a young man, being sixty-eight; my godmother was about
twenty years younger. In 1904 and 1905 he had traveled in this country
giving lectures, and may have met my godmother and her parents then.
Here are a few of his letters written to my godmother and found at Hill-
Stead:

May 14, 1911
Dear Miss Pope:
I seem to feel conscious of daring to presume to count (how is that for a
phrase?) on being able to have the pleasure of coming to you on Saturday
next 2nd, and I accordingly lose no more time in letting you know it. Would
it consort with your perfect convenience that I shall bring with me on Satur-
day, a very small and very humble-minded, very inoffensive and self-effacing
man (that likes *to "wash up" wherever he is!) little English servant of mine,*
on whom I in general rather depend, but with whom I can perfectly dispense
if your household can't easily make a corner for him?. . .He really quite helps
with the service wherever he is and perhaps wouldn't be a fifth wheel to the
coach (at least as far as I am concerned — even in such a generous establish-
ment as yours). I am looking forward with all joy to seeing you again and
your delightful parents to whom I send kindest remembrance.
Believe me, yours truly,
Henry James

Cambridge, Mass. 95 Irving Street
May 17, 1911
Dear Theodate Pope:
I have your very kind note and your telephone information just received. I
will take on Saturday the 12th, 6 o'clock train here for Hartford (with my
little attendant) and shall much appreciate being so handsomely met there.
Truly yours,
Henry James.

Towland House, Nahant, Mass.
June 16, 1911
My dear Theodate:
I have waited but to draw breath and somewhere free a few hours on end
to re-express to you more articulately my sense of that splendid service and

Theodate Pope Riddle / 54

Henry James, one of Hill-Stead's many distinguished guests.

55 / *Famous Visitors*

experience of Saturday and my more and more stored and settled gratitude for it. It was a wonderful and admirable day and one of those blest hours that abide with me always and become subjects to endless mental refiguring and overhauling, (past the wreath of impression or the fondness).

Your grateful friend,
Henry James.

Henry James was born on April 15, 1843, at five Washington Place, New York City. Henry's home life was "a place where ideas floated in freedom, tempered by humor and restricted by good sense. It was an atmosphere where speculation of some kind came easily. It was an environment in which writing something was as natural as planting corn in Iowa." (So said Henry Canby.) Henry James wished more than this idyllic family life, however, he wished to see something of the world, to get "impressions," and to know *people!* From age fifteen to twenty he lived with his family in Newport, Rhode Island, where he wrote his "Memoires," associating with the wealthy and the intellectuals there. In his teens he injured his back, was crippled for years, and could neither play sports nor join the army. As a result, he mingled with persons older than himself and assumed the role of "the Observer," often bedridden from pain, yet he determined to write. He never married, and the only woman he was really close to was his cousin, Minnie Temple, who died at an early age of tuberculosis. He found his friends among older women who were usually married.

He went to Harvard Law School but did not like Boston; yet, it was there that he met Charles Eliot Norton, who got him his first job, doing a series of travel sketches for *The Nation* in Europe. At this period, he became friends with William Dean Howells, who said of him: "A very earnest fellow—gifted enough to do better than anyone has done yet towards making a real American Novel."

He wrote twenty novels and twelve tales, all written in longhand and published as soon as finished. At twenty-five he was thought to be one of America's best storytellers; at thirty he was in Paris conferring with Turgenev, Flaubert, Zola, de Maupassant, and Daudet. At thirty-five he was famous and made his home in England, rarely returning to the United States except twice—once for a lecture tour and later, to visit Hill-Stead.

In 1915 he became a British subject, and the King bestowed upon him the rare Order of Merit a few months before he died. At the end of his life he said:

"I live, live intensely and am fed by life, and my value, whatever it may be is in my own kind of expression of that." He died in London at the age of seventy-three and is buried there.

James McNeill Whistler

Whistler is represented at Hill-Stead by his seventeen etchings that line the staircase, plus a few others. One in particular—*The Last of the Old Westminister Bridge* which Whistler called "a lithotint," done on stone—was a copy of an oil of his that my godmother sold to the Boston Museum of Fine Arts for $5,000.

Whistler also had four oil paintings at Hill-Stead: *The Blue Wave, Carmen Rossi* (both in the library), *Symphony in Violet and Blue* (in the dining room), and *The Beach at Selsey* (in the vestibule). Mr. Pope met and visited with Whistler in his studio in London and bought *The Blue Wave* which other museums throughout the world wished to buy. He purchased it for 1,000 pounds.

Another Connecticut patron of Whistler's was Harris Whittemore of Naugatuck, Connecticut, mentioned before. Mr. Whittemore bought Whistler's *Symphony in White No. 2,* the portrait of his first model, Jo Hefernen. (Carmen Rossi was his last model.)

Also, at the Hill-Stead library are books by Whistler: *The Gentle Art of Making Enemies, The Baronet and the Butterfly,* and others.

James McNeill Whistler was born on July 10, 1834, in Lowell, Massachusetts. His father, an army major, became a civil engineer and was assigned the task of building a railroad in Russia between St. Petersburg and Moscow. Before he was eleven, his family went to Russia. Whistler was sent to the Imperial Art Academy in St. Petersburg and did well. His family was given a large house overlooking the Neva River, and at night the boy would often leave his bed to gaze out the window at the spectacular fireworks over this river. In later years, his controversial painting, *The Falling Rocket,* was influenced by these early memories.

His father died in Russia, and his mother brought the two boys back to the United States, where they lived in Pomfret, Connecticut, so that the boys could attend the Pomfret School there. James was not good in his studies, except for his drawing. He was expelled for caricaturing the headmaster.

He then was sent to West Point but he did not fit in, due to his nearsightedness which made it hard for him to shoot a gun or ride a horse. He was dismissed, then got a job in Washington, D.C., for the United States Coast Guard Geodetic Survey, where he worked satisfactorily and

The elegant parlor bedroom, guest room of the famous.

learned to etch. In Washington he first went to parties and dances and found that he enjoyed social life and people in particular. Nevertheless, in February 1855 he decided to give up his post there, announcing to his family that he wished to go to Paris to study art. They agreed and at age twenty-one he left for Paris never to return to the United States.

In Paris he lived the bohemian life, on a very meager allowance from his family and made many friends among the artists. All his life, eating and sleeping were not as important as his art, and he worked for hours at a stretch. This dedication was hard on his models and others who often posed for seventeen hours and sometimes fainted.

One of his paintings, *The Falling Rocket,* or *Symphony in Red and Black,* was reviewed by John Ruskin, the famous British critic who gave it a bad notice. Ruskin called it "A poor excuse for throwing a pot of paint in the public's face." For this, Whistler brought suit and a notorious trial followed. News of it spread to the United States and Henry James covered it for his paper, *The Nation.* When the judge asked Whistler if 200 guineas was not a high price to pay for such a controversial painting, Whistler replied: "No! It was for the knowledge of a lifetime." This won applause from the court, and although he won the case, the court costs bankrupted him.

He loved London and spent much time there on the river Thames, which he sketched and painted in his famous *Nocturnes.* He painted his scenes from memory, after taking notes of what he saw and liked, using black and white chalk on brown paper. Returning home, he would paint them on canvas.

Whistler's last years were unproductive. His health was poor, his sight not good. His sister-in-law cared for him in her London home. He died at the age of sixty-nine in London on July 17, 1903, and is buried there.

8

Turning Points

MANY OF US experience turning points in our lives, usually without recognizing them as such at the time. This was true of my godmother when she met Mary Hillard, when she drew her first plans for Hill-Stead, when John Hillard died, and when she started purchasing land for Avon Old Farms School. Two more turning points were destined to influence her life further. The first was a brush with death in the icy waters of the North Atlantic, which had unhappy aftereffects; the second, her marriage to John Wallace Riddle, which brought fulfillment and happiness.

The Lusitania Episode

After her father's death in 1913, my godmother once more became interested in psychic research and communication with dear ones after death. This had been apparently successful after the death of John Hillard, but with her father there was no contact. This did not discourage her, and she planned to endow a chair in psychic phenomena at Harvard, headed by a Farmington resident, Mr. Edwin Friend, aged thirty-five, a scholar in this field. The chair never materialized due to unsatisfactory terms.

Nevertheless, in the spring of 1915 my godmother suddenly decided to sail to England on the *Lusitania,* taking Mr. Friend with her to see Sir Conan Doyle and others in this field. She wanted to discuss the possibility of publishing a magazine on the subject in the United States with Mr. Friend as its chief editor. She was invited to be the guest of Sir Oliver Lodge, a prominent English spiritualist.

Her mother, Mr. Friend, and her personal maid, whom she called "Robinson," went to New York together, where her mother said goodbye at the dock.

There had been threats that this ship would be sunk by German submarines, and most passengers had received warning telegrams but paid little attention to these "scare tactics." Only one man had a premonition that the ship would be sunk, and he canceled his trip a few days before the sailing date.

Many prominent persons were aboard including Charles Frohman, the famous theatrical producer, and Alfred Gwynne Vanderbilt. On the ship's passenger list my godmother was described as "An architect, a designer of libraries, Progressive Party Leader and psychical researcher." The captain described her as "Striking—in a severe way."

My godmother and Mr. Friend were finishing luncheon on that fateful day, May 7. An Englishman sitting near them had just ordered ice cream and laughingly remarked, "I hope it arrives before the Germans get us!" The orchestra in the dining room was playing "The Blue Danube," and it was still in the minds of my godmother and Mr. Friend when they went on deck for a stroll. The sea was bright blue and calm under a warm sun.

At that moment the torpedo struck. The ship began to list dangerously, and people crowded the deck, distraught, frightened, some in tears.

The "Lusitania" departs on her fateful last voyage.

They watched as the first lifeboat was loaded with passengers and lowered. Halfway down, it capsized, dropping its load into the sea where most of the occupants drowned.

My godmother's maid suddenly appeared at her side, her usual smile static on her frightened face. Aunt Theo put her hand on her shoulder and said, "Oh, Robinson!"

Soon the three went to A deck where lifeboats were being lowered safely and officers shouted frantic orders. Mr. Friend suggested that my godmother take her place in one of these boats, but she refused because Mr. Friend would not leave until all the women and children had been safely evacuated. She would not leave him.

The three of them decided to jump into the sea. Leaving Robinson for a few moments, my godmother and Mr. Friend procured life belts from the cabins near them, and Mr. Friend tied them on with good strong knots. Looking down, they could see the gray hull of the ship and knew that it was time to jump. My godmother asked Mr. Friend to go first, which he did. After a few seconds he surfaced and, looking up, encouraged my godmother and Robinson to follow him.

Aunt Theo then said: "Come, Robinson!" Climbing over the ropes, she jumped. She never saw either Mr. Friend or Robinson again.

Once in the water, my godmother could not rise to the surface and kept swallowing and breathing in salt water. She was not aware that she had been swept between decks. Closing her eyes, she decided that her life was over and prayed for her mother and Gordon and loved friends. She remembered all the buildings she had built and counted them, and then she said a wordless prayer to God, hoping her life had pleased Him.

Suddenly, she received a terrible blow on her head. She said afterward that her stiff hat and hair probably saved her from death. Then (evidently she had surfaced) she opened her eyes on a gray world with no color, due to the blow on her head. She was surrounded by hundreds of screaming, desperate humans. The ship had probably just sunk out of sight.

A man was clinging to her shoulders, pulling her under. He had no life belt and my godmother implored: "Oh, please don't." Then she became unconscious again.

When she finally surfaced she was floating on her back. There was only an old man near her. Asking him if he had seen any rescue boats, he replied: "No!" Spying a floating oar, she reached for it, pushed one end toward the old man, and then, as she felt her heavy, soaked clothes dragging her down, put her left leg over it and then her right. Doing this helped to save her. Floating uneasily, she looked about her and decided all this was a nightmare. Then she became unconscious again.

Her next wave of consciousness did not occur until four hours later, about 10:30 P.M. that evening. Opening her eyes, she saw a grate fire in the captain's cabin on board the rescue ship, *Julia*. Having temporarily forgotten the disaster, she wondered why she was lying on the floor wrapped in a blanket with hot stones at her feet and back. A man, staring at her and seeing her open her eyes, said, "She's conscious."

She had been saved by a nurse named Mrs. Naish, who watched sailors pull her on board the *Julia* with boat hooks. My godmother had been the last to be rescued and had been laid on the deck among the dead. Mrs. Naish, touching my godmother, said: "She feels like a sack of cement!" This was the result of being heavily soaked with salt water, but Mrs. Naish decided that my godmother could be saved and persuaded two men to work over her for two hours, after they had cut off her clothes using a carving knife brought from the dining saloon. She did not suffer when her breathing was restored, but soon a doctor arrived and ordered two sailors to carry her, making a chair with their hands. She was too weak to hold on, and the doctor held her as she was taken off the boat through the crowds on the dock. The sailors kept yelling: "Way! Way!" and then put her in an automobile and drove her to a third class hotel. Thinking that she could get out of the car, she fell flat on the sidewalk and was carried into a lounge filled with other passengers, all in borrowed clothes. The proprietress rushed to get her brandy. The Englishman, who had worried about his ice cream, came to sit beside her.

My godmother drank the brandy and then was helped upstairs to bed but she could have no peaceful sleep. She and her roommates were kept awake by men who came in, turning on lights, taking telegrams, bringing lost children for identification, and checking names for a list of survivors. She kept inquiring for Mr. Friend, but no one had seen him. Begging a Hartford man to search in hotels, hospitals, and private houses, he did and returned every two or three hours to report he had no news.

Three days later a married couple drove her to Cork. Here she rested and was treated for the fearful blow on her head which caused her to lose all her hair, so that for the rest of her life she was forced to wear a wig.

In August she went to Paris to visit Mary Cassatt and other friends and later returned to her home in Farmington. Most of her life, following this terrible experience, she was beset by fearful nightmares and could seldom sleep until 3:00 A.M. A devoted male cousin often walked with her up and down the halls of Hill-Stead trying to calm her.

My Godmother's Wedding

On May 6, 1916, a year and one day short of my godmother's rescue from the *Lusitania,* she married John Wallace Riddle, who had been ambassador to Russia under President Theodore Roosevelt. She had met him at the home of her friends, Admiral and Mrs. Sheffield Cowles of Farmington, and he had been wooing her for months. Tall, courtly, and her senior by a few years, he was a scholar in the field of history and diplomacy, and spoke six languages. At last, he persuaded her to marry him.

The wedding took place in The Cottage below Hill-Stead. Forty-eight guests attended this short ceremony in the small house. Those attending included Mrs. Pope; Gordon; my Aunt Mary Hillard; my mother and me; another godchild, Polly Wallace with her mother; my godmother's faithful secretary, Miss Elizabeth McCarthy; close friends from Farmington; helpers at the Gundy; and the whole staff from Hill-Stead, including the men who worked in the fields and barns.

Time dragged while we waited for Aunt Theo to arrive. Her future husband appeared nervous. Mrs. Pope began to feel faint in the close atmosphere, and Mary Hillard kept holding a bottle of smelling salts to her nose. Little Gordon, Aunt Theo's foster son, now aged three was leaning against Mrs. Pope and became restless.

Finally, my Aunt Mary said to John Riddle, "John, I think you had better go up and *fetch* Theo." Eagerly he left, soon to return with a ra-

The wedding guests

diant Theodate on his arm. (Later, Aunt Theo confided to me in a whisper that she *never* would have come to her wedding if Uncle John Riddle had not gone up to "fetch" her!)

After the short but beautiful ceremony we all walked up to the front lawn of Hill-Stead to have our pictures taken. Then followed a happy reception party with fabulous refreshments, after which the newlyweds drove away for their honeymoon.

They were devoted to each other until the end of their lives—he dying first. Unfortunately, the newlyweds experienced some harrowing events whenever they traveled by ship. Aunt Theo was known to sailors as "a regular Jonah." Often seamen refused to sign up if she was listed as a passenger. In Norway, for example, their boat ran onto rocks and all had to abandon ship. When the Riddles reached Southampton for their voyage home, their vessel caught fire and burned the day before departure. On Aunt Theo's return from the Argentine in 1922 the boat's rudder jammed, causing it to circle out of control and almost capsizing in the process. After this, she never traveled by sea again. It was as though the ocean felt angry and frustrated that it had not been able to possess her during her *Lusitania* experience and close escape from death.

Although my godmother and her John were separated by their respective responsibilities for long periods of time, they were always very much in love and readjusted to each other when reunited at Hill-Stead.

... May 6, 1916.

Ambassador John Wallace Riddle at Hill-Stead.

Theodate Pope Riddle / 66

The Final Years

IN 1920 John Riddle was appointed ambassador to the Argentine, and Aunt Theo accompanied him to his post. After staying a few months she returned to the United States because her plans for Avon Old Farms School had crystallized, and she was eager to start construction, having acquired the thousands of acres she felt would be required for the school.

Avon Old Farms School

For years she had believed that the present generation of young people needed "a foundation of education that will teach them to know the out-of-doors and lead them to a choice of life vocation that will suit their abilities and serve their future success." In addition to the regular academic courses taught in high school, Avon included carpentry and printing shops, a forge, a working farm, and other facilities for teaching various trades. Aunt Theo wanted the school to cater to the needs of each student because "the ways in which people differ are more important than the ways they are alike."

Working with leading educators of the day, she evolved a carefully thought out plan of education which was essentially progressive. It contrasted with the school's architecture, which was picturesque and traditional. A combination of English Cotswold architecture and elements of her own previous work, the design of the twenty-five buildings was essentially her own artistic creation with curving and sweeping roofs and walls which, when added to the overall effect, gave the design an individuality of its own.

She spent much of her time during the next five years on the site, personally supervising the workmen (numbering as many as 250 at one time) who were encouraged to use old tools and processes in constructing the buildings. Aunt Theo described her construction method as follows:

Before starting this work all trades were advised that inasmuch as the effectiveness of these buildings would depend to a very great extent upon the way the various surfaces were finished, it was most important that the workers dispense with all mechanical methods and wherever possible, use old tools and processes in carrying out the work. They were instructed to work by rule of thumb and to gauge all verticals by eye; as a natural variation in line and surface was far more desirable in this work than accuracy.

In 1927 the school opened with 140 students and a staff of approximately 20, headed by a provost in charge of the faculty. Aunt Theo devised a student government based on that of a New England town, with laws and governmental functions administered regularly and officers elected semiannually from the student body.

World War II brought more problems for the school than my aunt could cope with. John Riddle had died in 1941, leaving Aunt Theo desolate. The school closed finally in 1944 and was taken over immediately by the army as a rehabilitation center for blind veterans and did not reopen

Headmaster's house, Avon School.

Architectural detail, Avon School.

69 / *The Final Years*

Architectural detail, Avon School.

until two years later. Since that time it has enjoyed great success, although its curriculum has had to be modified somewhat to meet the changing needs of later times.

Aunt Theo's Last Years

During the depression years of the 1930s my aunt maintained her household as before and, with her husband back at Farmington, continued her usual entertaining schedule. It was during this time when I was in my teens that Aunt Theo remarked to me solemnly, "I can't get along without two butlers!" I, who had never had a butler in my family, found it hard to suppress a smile.

"I've found a *new* butler to help Ernest," she continued. "The other one left, as you know. This young man is Russian — born of Russian nobility. Your Uncle John Riddle knew his family in Russia when your Uncle John was serving as ambassador to Russia before I was married to him. This young man escaped during the Revolution and finally managed to get to Hill-Stead, hoping to work for me. He knows nothing about any

Refectory steps, Avon School.

kind of work, but said he was sure he could be a butler! So—I think you'll like him. He is in his twenties and is an intellectual. He begged me to let him stay here. He said: 'In this beautiful place—I'll do *anything* to help you!' "

He became the most prestigious butler Aunt Theo ever had. His manners were of royal vintage, and the way he opened the front door to guests had Ernest regarding him with wonder, shaking his head! The way he helped me into my coat was like an embrace, and everyone was charmed by "Alex," as he called himself.

Yes! Aunt Theo knew how to make *everyone* happy!

Illness and Death

In 1945 it was evident to me that my godmother had become ill and was no longer able to entertain as she so loved to do. I had returned to Hartford, and Aunt Theo came several times to see my new baby son and to confer with my father, who was a lawyer. Preoccupied with personal problems, I was unaware of the length of time which had elapsed since her last visit. I was astonished to learn that she had become desperately

The Makeshift Theater at Hill-Stead, used by Avon students.

ill with cancer, died, and been buried in the Sunken Garden under her favorite pine tree.

Her choice of a final resting place was not to be, however. The Town of Farmington informed the Hill-Stead trustees that "it is unlawful for anyone to be buried in their own yard. Burial must be in the town cemetery." Accordingly, my Aunt Theo's body was moved to a plot near the Farmington River on a bluff in this cemetery. On one side of her lies Gordon Brockway; on the other, Ernest Bohlen.

She who had loved so greatly was laid to rest with no one dear to her at the brief, terse service. Not one of her relatives nor foster sons could attend her funeral; they were miles away, on the West Coast, in Africa, and in Canada. Again I, who lived so close by, had not been informed.

The mystic initials, JIL, were never carved on her flat tombstone.

Theodate in 1946, the year of her death.

Epilogue

"Here at Hill-Stead is simple beauty. Yes, acreage bountiful, but to walk on the porch and gaze over the valley one can feel life here. It is not a dead museum, but a home for all time." Alan R. Hunter has given us this sense of Hill-Stead's immorality. However permanent it may appear, more than an ample endowment is needed to preserve and maintain such an establishment. Only unceasing human dedication, concern, and devotion will safeguard the material and spiritual quality of such a heritage.

Since my godmother's death Hill-Stead has been blessed by the help of Mrs. Milo Dotson, the competent housekeeper, and her assistant, Ingrid Carlson. In addition, Allen Peck, the faithful caretaker, has had sole charge of all work on the grounds and buildings, work which he performs alone. Three curators have also perpetuated Hill-Stead's traditions and interpreted them to the public.

The Curators

The Frisbies, who were the first curators, kept everything just as it was when my godmother lived there. The Watsons, deciding that living on the third floor in the main building was too difficult (they were near retirement age), obtained permission from the trustees to tear out the great old kitchen, making a place for their living room-dining room combination. Their bedrooms were on the second floor above this, where the maids used to live. They also changed the location of a few of the paintings. Monet's beautiful oil of *The Bay of Antibes* they moved from its original location over the fireplace in the Ell Room to above the fireplace in the living room. One of the two *Haystacks* by Monet was moved from over the fireplace in the living room to the Ell Room. *The Tub,* by Degas, a pastel, was switched from the parlor-bedroom to the living room. Aunt

75

Mementos of the famous.

Theo had a good reason for her original positioning of these pictures. The Ell Room had been color-designed to enhance *The Bay of Antibes;* its drapes and wallpaper blended with this painting. This gave entering guests a long perspective that drew them forward to Aunt Theo, who always stood near it to greet her friends. *The Haystacks* paintings were purposely hung near each other for comparison, which enthralled the guests. *The Tub* (a naked girl washing her feet in a small tin tub) was appropriate for the parlor-bedroom, not the living room.

The Gerald Talbots, the recently retired curators, were devoted and helpful in every way. Mr. Talbot, extremely erudite and well informed in the arts, knew the background of all the paintings and objets d'art at Hill-Stead, and both he and his wife were excellent artists in their own right, painting beautiful pictures in whatever spare time they could gather from their long hours of supervision at the museum. Neither aged since their arrival many years ago, just as those who live for any length of time at Hill-Stead never age. My godmother always looked exactly the same to the end of her life; and Ernest, the butler, never looked older, nor did any of the others. Why is this? One can only surmise that it is due to the beauty, peace, and happiness found at Hill-Stead, along with excellent food, clean water, fresh country air, and congenial companionship.

Late in the summer of 1982 the Hill-Stead trustees hired a new set of curators, Ursula and Philip Wright, a competent, careful, and devoted couple.

The Sixth Sense

Aunt Theo was always interested in psychic research and was a psychic herself. She was sensitive to my needs. Without warning, her chauffeur-driven car would arrive at our house, the chauffeur would knock and announce to me: "The madame wishes you to come to Hill-Stead at once!"

"Oh, Charles! I've just washed my hair, and it isn't dry yet!"

"Then I'll sit and wait for you!"

How did my Aunt Theo know that I had been depressed? That I *needed* the peace and tranquility of Hill-Stead at that very moment? I would go there and be surrounded by "the peace that passeth all understanding" and be cured of my youthful depression.

Aunt Theo was also psychic about Hill-Stead. Once, while in a hotel in New York City, she suddenly awoke to see visionary flames on the wall of her bedroom. She called Hill-Stead, and Ernest answered the telephone at 2:00 A.M. Before my godmother could question him, he said, "Yes, Miss Pope, we have just put out the fire in the wastebasket!"

I too have this gift of extrasensory perception and, on many occasions, have perceived when a close friend or relative was in danger. Since Hill-Stead has meant so much to me, it is natural that I should have had intuitive feelings concerning it.

In October 1950 I had just been driven home from Gloucester, Massachusetts, by a kind Scotch-Irish woman who insisted on doing this for me after I returned from the hospital, having nearly died from a ruptured appendix. One beautiful morning I had a distinct feeling that Hill-Stead was in danger. Since I never go against my intuitions, I said:

"Mrs. H, I must go to Hill-Stead at once!"

"*What!* An' how can ye drive? Ye can no drive?"

"I *can* drive, and I've *got* to go! Will you go with me?"

"Sure, 'n ye don't think I'd be lettin' ye go way out there alone?"

I was very weak, but I managed to drive, going slowly.

When we reached Hill-Stead the two curators were sitting on the front porch. As they saw me walking feebly toward them, they arose and ran to meet me.

Greeting me with hugs and kisses, they told me:

"Thank God you have come! Something *terrible* is happening!"

"What—*what?*" I asked.

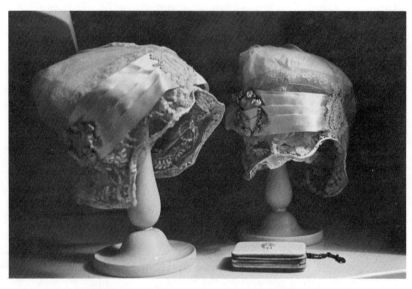

Reminders of an era of elegance.

"That cousin of Mrs. Riddle's has been here selling *all* the silver and linens! He says he's going to tear down Hill-Stead and give the money to Avon Old Farms! He says he'll sell *all* the paintings!" and they wept.

"I'll do something — right away!" I promised. "I'll get my friend, Catherine Day, to help. She's Harriet Beecher Stowe's great niece and *loves* Hill-Stead!"

Driving back was not easy, but we made it, and I telephoned Miss Day at once. She was horrified.

"We'll get my good friend, Anson McCook," she said. "He has never lost a case yet. We will fight it through the courts if *you* will testify. We'll *save* Hill-Stead!"

We fought it in court and *won!* Then this same disgruntled cousin, who had always boasted that Aunt Theo would leave Hill-Stead to *him,* tried to demolish it a second time. Everyone helped thwart this attempt, and now we hope that Hill-Stead will be safe for all time.

While Hill-Stead stands, the gracious buildings will continue to memorialize one of the twentieth century's most unusual women, an outstanding architect, an imaginative educational innovator, a benefactress of young people, and above all a lover of mankind. Truly her name Theodate, "Gift of the Gods," was well chosen.

I found a framed poem in my godmother's bedroom at Hill-Stead. It is unsigned, illuminated, British in character, yet to me it expresses the epitome of Hill-Stead during my godmother's life there. This might have been written by Henry James as a thank you note to my godmother.

For morning sun and evening dew,
For every bud that April knew,
For storm and silence, gloom and light,
And for the solemn stars at night.
For fallow field and burdened byre,
For rooftree and the hearthside fire,
For everything that shines and sings,
For dear familiar daily things —
The friendly trees, and in the sky
The white cloud squadron sailing by.
For Hope that waits and Faith that dares,
For Patience that still smiles and bears;
For Love that fails not nor withstands;
And healing touch of children's hands —
For happy labour, high intent,
For all life's blessed sacrament.
O Comrad of our nights and days
Thou givest all things, take our praise!

Bountiful acreage and simple beauty.

Illustrations

All photographs in this volume were taken by John K. Atticks, III, with the exception of early pictures of individuals and events, and those identified in the captions as being taken by Theodate Pope Riddle. In the following, each illustration is listed in the order in which it appears. The small, uncaptioned photographs which embellish the chapter titles are listed only if they are not repeated later in the chapter on a larger scale.

INDEX

My Godmother
Theodate Pope Riddle
has been published in a first edition
of fifteen hundred copies.
Designed by A. L. Morris,
the text was composed in Garamond
and printed by Courier Printing Company
in Littleton, New Hampshire, on Mohawk Vellum Text.
Endleaves were printed by Courier on
Strathmore Americana Text,
and the binding in James River Graphics Kivar
was executed by New Hampshire Bindery
in Concord, New Hampshire.